The Critical Path Career

How to Advance in Construction Planning and Scheduling

Micah Piippo, Greg Lawton

Beyond Deadlines

Contents

HOW TO MAKE MORE MONEY

Welcome to a pivotal turning point in your career in Construction Planning and Scheduling. This book is your guide to earning more annually in your role. When my journey began, the landscape was vastly different. Technical know-how was limited. Pathways to career advancement did not exist.

Fast forward to today, and technical information is available in abundance. The internet is filled with technical guidance. Countless hours of training and in-depth guides on YouTube exist. AI agents can even provide step-by-step instructions.

However, a critical gap remains: there's not enough information on career progression.

That's why I created this book.

To provide you with a guide to help you earn more money through career progression. I provide specific steps based on the situation you are in. This wasn't intended to be read from start to finish. Feel free to skip directly to your current stage in life.

MONEY IS A BIG DEAL

Let's take two people, for example. Bill and Lindsey. Both start out making $100K per year. Bill decides to never leave his job or ask for a raise. After getting raises in years 3 and 7, Lindsey eventually makes $200K.

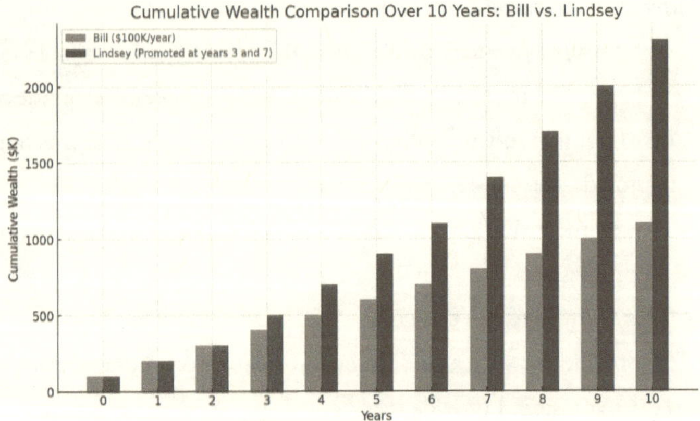

Over that 10-year period, Lindsey will make **$1.2 million dollars more**. Who would you rather be? Bill or Lindsey? If you want to be Lindsey, keep reading.

I think money is a big deal because it provides more options.

You can have more family vacations, spend on education, or retire early. You can also use these tactics and strategies to be more hybrid or remote, increase your paid time off, work on projects that interest you, and pretty much any other desire you have.

Money Isn't a Big Deal

Money as a measure of success is a horrible idea. At a certain point, **earning more money could have diminishing returns**. You begin to sacrifice things you care more about.

The extra money isn't worth it. For example, there's no money in the world that can give you more time with your family. Or bring back the time when you had perfect health. Take time to work out your salary goal.

When will enough be enough? What are some of the other priorities in your life that wouldn't be worth the extra money?

PLANNER VS SCHEDULER

In different parts of the world, the role of Planner and the role of Scheduler can mean different things. So I don't have to keep using the phrase Planner or Scheduler; from here on out, I'm going to simply say Scheduler. I've worked and hired people all over the world.

These tactics and strategies work for everyone in planning and scheduling.

Five Ways to Make More Money

There are only five ways to make more money as a scheduler.

1. Get a raise

2. Get promoted.

3. Get a new job that pays more.

4. Get more clients or charge more.

5. Create software or products and sell them higher than the production cost.

Getting you a raise will typically bring you the least amount of money, getting a promotion will pay you more, getting a new job will pay you more, and owning your own consultancy or creating your own software will give you an unlimited amount of earnings.

Getting a raise is the easiest, getting a new job is harder, and starting your own consultancy is the hardest.

I will cover starting a consultancy and creating software in another book because there is simply too much there to cover. I have organized the next sections based on what you are looking for. Skip to the section that makes the most sense for you.

You'll notice there are repetitive steps across each scenario.

Skip around to find what you need.

How to Get a Raise

Getting a raise in Planning and Scheduling is largely influenced by your direct supervisor. While they make the decision, it's your job to influence the decision. A raise is typically a one-time increase in salary. Companies will have a structured or unstructured process for raises.

Step 0 - Figure Out The Process

Your first task is to figure out if your company has a structured process. Structured means there is a set period every year, there are standard forms, there's a standard process, and everyone is doing the same thing. Structured also means there are set amounts that are given.

Unstructured means there's next to nothing to explain how you get a raise at the company. Which means you'll need to create the structure to get a raise.

Keep in mind different people will be in different stages. Below is a typical process for asking for a raise. If you've been a top performer for some time and are in an unstructured process, you may just need to ask.

Skip to step 4 and go get that raise.

Step 1 - Communicate Early That You Want a Raise

The best strategy is to communicate as far in advance as you can to your manager that salary is one of the most important parts of your compensation package.

Be clear that you'd like to pursue a raise.

Questions like, "How are raises determined?" and "What types of accomplishments do people in my role achieve to receive raises?" Or "Since there isn't a standard process, how do you generally approach raises? I've done some salary research, and based on that data, there should be some growth in my position and would like to share it."

This initial conversation is a fact-finding mission for you to determine more details about the process. It also plants a seed in your manager's mind so there are no surprises down the road. At the end of the conversation, ask if it's okay to check in on this topic on a monthly basis to the regular one-on-one syncs.

Step 2 - Establish a Regular Sync

You have now opened a space where you can talk about compensation every month. If raises are decided in November and it's currently January, you now have 10 months to influence your manager's decision. In most cases, you should meet with your manager weekly or biweekly. Set aside one of those meetings per month to discuss the raise.

The best way to influence your manager's decision is to establish a set of expectations and then exceed them. In your first couple of syncs, work with your manager to figure out what those expectations are.

Keep in mind that it will always remain somewhat ambiguous. Doing A+B+C won't necessarily equal a raise. Figuring out what A, B, and C are will, however, allow you to focus your energy and time on tasks.

Step 3 - Demonstrate
Measurable Progress

Create and maintain a list of the tasks and achievements. Prior to each sync you've scheduled with your manager to talk about a raise, take time to prepare ahead of the conversation.

At the beginning of the meeting with your manager, make it clear that the topic is a raise. Don't dive into the details of what you've been doing immediately. This can shift the conversation into work details instead of the raise.

Try to align on the big items you agreed to at the start of the process. You can say, "I've been working on A+B+C, and want to check that these are still the efforts that will put me in a position for a raise?". Most often, your manager will say yes. Then, share a couple of big wins in those areas.

Business priorities change. As I mentioned before, it's not always A+B+C that you automatically get a raise. If priorities do change, go tackle them head-on. Also, look for ways to add extra wins to your effort. Remember you are trying to exceed your manager's expectations.

I get you might be loaded up 110%. But your manager and the company will always have lots of problems. Find the right problem, think creatively, and you can find something that, with very little effort, you can add as a big win.

Lastly, these syncs should be pointing to a specific point where you ask for the raise. In a structured process, this will be well known. For example, each October, performance reviews and raises happen. In an unstructured process, you'll need to create this timeline. You'll have to say, "Do you think we'll have enough performance to consider me for a raise by October?"

Step 4 - Ask For The Raise

You have spent weeks and months crushing it at work. The wins have started to stack up. Whatever timeline you've established with your boss or that your company has, you're near the end of it.

In one of your one-on-ones with your manager, say, "As we discussed at the beginning of the year, A, B, and C were tremendously important to you for me to complete. I was able to complete those and even got to D and E, which were stretch goals. I'd consider myself a top performer, but would appreciate your feedback."

Often, slam dunk, and you walk about with a nice % bump in pay. If it doesn't work out your way, don't fret. You can always try again, go for a promotion that includes a raise, or go get a new job.

How to Get Promoted

B e careful; not all promotions include salary raises. If you accept more responsibility and do more work for the same salary, you've effectively gotten the opposite of a raise and are losing money.

Step 0 - Figure Out The Process

Each company will have a promotion process that ranges from very structured to completely informal. Figure out what exists at your company.

Some companies have structured career ladders that specifically state the expectations for the next role.

Some companies have specific time frames in which you can be promoted. Other companies have nothing, so it's up to you to figure it out.

Step 1 – Show Interest
& Start a Career Con-
versation

Way ahead of when you want your promotion, ask your manager in a one-on-one what a promotion in this role would look like. What is the process? What are the expectations? How long does it take?

Leverage what you've learned about the process ahead of time to ask thoughtful questions. Close the conversation by asking if you can set up a regular career conversation.

Step 2 - Build a
Roadmap of Skills and
Experiences

Start with understanding the essential skills of your job before aiming higher.

This could mean mastering Primavera P6 and deeply understanding the project you are building, then moving on to handling more projects for the company.

When picking skills and experiences, look to model people you know who have been promoted. If there isn't an example, look to your manager and her peers for examples.

Step 3 - Build Strate-
gic Relationships That
Matter

Promotion is heavily influenced by people. It might help to think of it as a popularity contest. Often, numerous people have to review and approve promotions. As you get into your promotion journey, look to secure 3 strategic relationships:

A Mentor: This should be someone who is slightly ahead of you in a similar career path and can provide practical advice and insights.

A Cross-Functional Peer: This is a fellow colleague of yours at the same level but in a different department, such as project management or cost estimation. They can help you better understand how scheduling impacts other areas of the business.

Your Manager's Manager: This is someone who holds a higher position in the organizational hierarchy than your own manager. Engage with them quarterly or semi-annually to discuss project updates and strategic insights, helping you stay visible to upper management.

Setting up these relationships isn't a one-time effort. You must continually work to maintain these relationships. As you move closer to promotion, it's key that these individuals are aware of your plans and advocating on your behalf.

Step 4 - Demonstrate Impact

Impact is a result that far exceeds expectations that have been set for you. Consider the following scenario:

Who do you think has a better chance of getting promoted?

Person A, "I enter the status the project manager provides and then I create and share the reports as instructed."

Person B, "I saved the project 3 weeks by reviewing the status the project manager had provided and analyzing it for opportunities."

Delivering impact requires you to know what your expectations are, what the goals of the project are, and what the goals of the company are. You are not some superhuman machine that will deliver all of those. But, your focus and time can be aligned with something that matters to the people above you.

Typically, most impact needs to be translated into dollars. For example, 3 weeks of schedule savings could be converted into dollars. You could add the overheads and the cost of work.

Remember that you will need to share your impact for people to realize you've made an impact. Bring it up with your manager, share it in your manager's manager meeting, and bring it up in team meetings. Push through the anxiety to share. People are enormously busy and heavily distracted these days.

Missing your great work will be extremely easy if you aren't bringing it up.

Step 5 - Directly Ask for the Promotion

You will never get what you don't ask for. Having reached this point, you have a very compelling case to advance.

In a 1v1 with your manager, state your key accomplishments to date. Compare how they match and exceed the next level you are trying to be promoted to. Ask to be put forward for a promotion.

Then, be quiet and let your manager respond.

You will probably be super nervous. Nervous people tend to ramble and over-communicate. That's why I recommend keeping it short and then allowing your manager to respond.

Step 6 - You Didn't Get
It

While I worked at Google, one of my coworkers went for a promotion 7 times before he got it. If you are turned down, take it as an opportunity to improve.

Figure out the reasoning behind it. There are typically 2 factors that prevent promotion. You didn't demonstrate enough impact to show you are ready for the next level. For example, when you are not seen leading enough scheduled status update meetings, these are areas where you can focus your efforts for improvement. The next isn't a role available right now. This is completely out of your control.

There is a point where, for whatever reason, a promotion at the company isn't an option. If that is the case, and you still want to earn more money, then your next option is to find a new job.

How to Land a New Job

Getting a new job can change your career trajectory. Too often, people sit in jobs after they've learned everything the role can provide. After earning every raise and promotion possible.

Think back to the earlier Bill and Lindsey scenario. For the vast majority of Planners and Schedulers stay in a role too long. This caps your potential earnings.

Step 0 - Prepare Yourself

Applying for new jobs is a numbers game. You will spend quite a bit of time getting that cover letter ready, polishing your resume, and entering all that information into the application. Then, you will be rejected. And rejected. And potentially rejected again.

Similar to riding a bike, some people get it on the first try, while others fall over and over again. Others find that a scooter works best for them.

Preparing yourself for rejection will create a much better mindset for the process.

Step 1 - Establish Preferences

When looking for a job, it is easy to waste time looking at jobs you will never apply for. Since this is a numbers game, you want to spend most of your time on high-value-added tasks.

You can optimize your search and application process by defining a couple of things upfront. It creates a set of filters. This will save loads of time.

You can add more than these, but I would recommend starting at least these three.

- Where do you want to work

- What role do you want to have

- How much do you want to be paid

For example, I would work anywhere in California, Texas, or New York. Based on my experience, I'm seeking a Project Controls Manager or Scheduling Manager role - total compensation over $200K.

Understanding Compensation

Companies have a variety of methods to compensate their employees. Most people are used to salary or base pay. There are bonuses, equity, commissions (not typical for construction), and benefits.

In my experience, many big tech companies' salaries will be a bit lower than the market's, but they will make up for the delta with equity. Remember, bonuses and equities aren't typically guaranteed.

You want to establish a minimum base pay or salary level that you would require to move jobs.

Step 2 - Identify Ideal Companies

If you are going to land a new job, why not at least try to shoot for one of the best at first? I've found that this is also a great way to build your package (resume, cover letter, LinkedIn Profile, referral).

At the time of writing this book, below are some of the top companies. Examples of Tech Companies with Large Construction Programs

Google

Microsoft

Amazon

Meta

Intel

Next, top Construction Companies. Depending on where you are, this will have a bit of a regional flair, but the steps will remain the same. I find the ENR reports to be easy to use. Below is a slice of their Top 400 Contractors of 2023 ranked by construction revenue.

The Turner Corp

Bechtel

MasTec

Kiewit Corp

STO Building Group

<u>DPR Construction</u>

<u>The Whiting-Turner Contracting Co.</u>

<u>Fluor</u>

<u>Clark Group</u>

<u>Skanska USA</u>

<u>Hensel Phelps</u>

<u>Gilbane Building Co.</u>

There are a variety of other lists out there. Simply Google 'Top General Contractors', and you'll be able to find what you are looking for.

Step 3 - Identify Jobs to Apply For

Depending on your location, LinkedIn will primarily be the source for the job postings you are looking for. The first step is to figure out the right job titles for which you are searching. Using the job search in LinkedIn, an entry to mid-level scheduler might use the below Job Titles to find jobs;

- Scheduler

- Construction Scheduler

- P6 Scheduler

- Planner

- Construction Planner

- Primavera P6

A senior person looking for a managerial role might try the following Job Titles;

- Schedule Manager

- Scheduling Manager

- Planning and Scheduling Manager

- Project Controls Manager

- Planning Manager

The key is to try a couple of different searches until you've found a selection of jobs that fit what you are looking for. Open up the job postings and read through them. Make sure these align with what you are looking for. It's okay if certain jobs don't fit your location or salary criteria.

Do the responsibilities look like what you are interested in doing? Do you meet 70% of the job posting requirements?

Once you've found the right fit, use the Job Title and apply your criteria. It could be Project Controls Manager, California, Texas, New York, $200K+ salary. If no jobs appear, try adjusting the salary or modifying the job titles.

If still no jobs appear, don't fret. Setup job alerts for your searches. You'll be notified when jobs appear in your area and can apply for them.

Step 4 - Apply to Jobs

You've found that perfect job; now it's time to apply.

Here's some bad news... There's a good chance you won't get it. You'll spend all that time preparing your resume and filling out the application. And then you won't even get a call back. But here's also some good news for you... If done correctly, that time spent won't be a waste.

You'll be able to use 85% of what you did on the next job. Keep that in mind as we walk through this next section.

Prior to applying, ensure you have the following 4 items prepared.

1. Referral

2. Resume

3. Cover Letter

4. LinkedIn Profile

Referral

The job market at these companies is extremely competitive. Without a referral, it's even harder. People are generally motivated to refer because they get paid if their referrals are hired. Don't be afraid to ask someone for a referral. I've been asked for countless blind referrals, and almost always, I'm more than happy to submit them.

When asking for a referral, always ask for the referral before applying for the job. Often, if you apply to the job first, the person will lose out on their potential for a referral bonus.

Resume

You want recruiters or hiring managers to read your resume for 60 seconds and immediately think, "I need to call this person".

As a Project Controls and Scheduling Manager, I've reviewed thousands of resumes. You'd be surprised how many people submit unorganized, unclear, and poorly structured resumes.

With the tools and services available today, there's no excuse not to have a top resume.

To get you started, is an editable copy of my resume.

Several top companies have interviewed me and hired me based on this resume.

You can also find numerous free templates online with a Google search.

Templates help visually, but content is still necessary.

Your content will be unique to your background and the job you are applying for.

Don't forget to emphasize your impact, preferably in numbers.

Rather than stating that you updated 15 schedules, describe a time when you encountered an 8-week delay or found a way to save time.

Here are some additional resources to consider watching.

- https://www.youtube.com/watch?v=Tt08KmFfIYQ

- https://www.youtube.com/watch?v=MqXjqOy-TA8

- https://www.youtube.com/watch?v=sgnN2jxka1E

Cover Letter

Cover letters have always been a struggle for me to the point that I stopped writing them altogether.

Insert AI, cover letters are back for me. [M2]

Here is an easy-to-follow video on how to draft your cover letter.
https://www.youtube.com/watch?v=pmnY5V16GSE

LinkedIn Profile

Recruiters and hiring managers will often look at your LinkedIn. For very little time, you can have a top-tier LinkedIn profile. Below are a couple of resources;

- https://www.youtube.com/watch?v=BcfGWi8Qywk

- https://www.youtube.com/watch?v=2ZvPos2c_bg

Step 5 - Land the Job

Over the years, I've interviewed hundreds of schedulers. I've been interviewed countless times. I did well in some interviews and not so well in others. And it came down to practice.

Not practicing is the biggest mistake you can make. Don't expect to get hired if you ramble on for 15 minutes when asked, "Tell me about yourself." Don't expect to be hired if you talk so fast that it sounds like you are being played at 1.75x speed. Don't expect to be hired if you cannot name one of the company's construction projects or explain how it's built.

Step 6 - Post Interview

Congratulations, you made it through the wringer. Now, it's up to others to decide if you're the right fit. I strongly recommend sending a thank you note. Here is an excellent guide on how to do it.

- https://www.youtube.com/watch?v=gSbV3q_MMbg

I'd also recommend taking stock of the experience. There's a good chance you still won't get the job. It's simply how this game works. However, you can always use this as an opportunity to improve. What question could you have done better on? Is there a key skill or experience missing from your package? Add it.

INTERVIEW QUESTIONS

Below are a set of questions that we have used to interview hundreds of the world top schedulers. A few points before you dive in. Job interviews can make anyone feel anxious. **Practice helps calm the nerves.** When you are interviewing, you want your answers to flow naturally and that only happens with practice. As a general rule, keep your answers under 2 minutes. Keep an eye on the interviewer to see if they are still tracking during longer answers. You can always ask "Would you like me to expand on this"?

Use the examples as a guide and add your own thoughts. Try to not make stuff up on the spot. Write down 5 to 6 work experiences that you can reference in a variety of ways. When going through the below questions, figure out how you can pull from these 5 or 6. It's ok to pause and think prior to answering a question. Try not barrel into answering. You'll end up speaking too quickly and losing the interviewer. Always be truthful, no lying.

General Questions

1. Why do you want to work in construction scheduling, and what motivated you to pursue this career path?

How to Answer: Talk about your passion for planning, coordinating, and problem-solving, and how these are essential skills in construction scheduling. Discuss your fascination with the construction process and how scheduling plays a critical role in making a project successful. You might also mention any early experiences, such as a relevant degree or mentor, that directed you towards this path.

Example: From a young age, I was fascinated by the process of constructing a building – it's like assembling a massive puzzle where all pieces need to fit perfectly. My education in civil engineering further propelled this interest, and after my first role in a construction project, I found scheduling to be the part where I could make the most impact. I love the challenge of crafting a detailed and workable plan and then seeing it help a project come to life efficiently and effectively.

2. What do you know about our company, and why do you think you would be a good fit here?

How to Answer: Prior to the interview, research the company's history, projects, culture, and values. Use this information to tie your skills and experience to the company's needs and culture. Name drop a CEO or Vice President.

Example: I know that your company has a strong reputation for delivering high-quality commercial projects on time and under budget. Your commitment to sustainable building practices is something that I deeply respect. In my previous role, I reduced project delivery times by an average of 15% through effective scheduling, which I believe aligns with your company's emphasis on efficiency.

3. What skills or qualities do you have that would make you successful in this role?

How to Answer: Be specific and give examples. Talk about your technical skills (such as proficiency with scheduling software), your attention to detail, your ability to foresee potential delays and create contingency plans, and your excellent communication skills.

Example: I am highly proficient in using Primavera P6 and MS Project, which allows me to create detailed and accurate schedules. My strong analytical skills help me to foresee potential issues and develop contingency plans. I'm also a great communicator, which I believe is key in coordinating between various stakeholders and ensuring everyone is aligned with the schedule.

4. How do you handle deadlines and prioritize tasks when managing multiple projects at the same time?

How to Answer: Discuss your organizational and time management strategies. Emphasize your ability to remain calm under pressure, to prioritize tasks effectively and to work with others. Mention a strategy like the . Drop tools you use, such as Slack, Smartsheets, and Google Sheets.

Example: To manage critical work, I prefer to use the Eisenhower matrix and smartsheets. By combining them, I stay in excellent communication with my teammates and avoid dropping the ball. One example was when I was rolling out updated contractual requirements across all of our global projects and a project I was scheduling was delayed. I was able to deliver the contracts and support the project by prioritizing what was absolutely critical and urgent. There were also other tasks that I didn't have bandwidth for and had to ask for help to cover.

5. Can you describe your experience working in a team environment and your approach to collaboration?

How to Answer: Highlight your experience working with different professionals (e.g., architects, contractors, and clients) and how you successfully navigated those relationships. Emphasize your approach to teamwork, your communication skills, and your willingness to listen and compromise to achieve the best outcome for the project.

Example: In my previous role, I worked closely with architects, contractors, and clients. I made it a priority to establish open and frequent communication channels with all team members. I believe in actively listening to everyone's concerns and ideas, and I'm willing to adapt the schedule as needed while maintaining the project's objectives. One specific instance was when we faced an unexpected supply delay; I facilitated a brainstorming session with the team, and we collaboratively re-sequenced the work to keep the project on track without compromising the quality.

Remember, the goal of your answers is not just to show your competence, but also to demonstrate your passion for the role, your familiarity with the company, and your readiness to contribute positively to the team and projects at hand.

Hypothetical Questions

6. If a client requested a project deadline that you believed was unrealistic, how would you handle the situation?

How to Answer: Explain that you would evaluate the entire scope of work and identify critical paths in the schedule. Clearly and professionally communicate your concerns with the client, backed with data and propose an alternative, more realistic timeline. Mention the importance of negotiating and potentially compromising to find a middle ground.

Example: On a recent hospital project, the client wanted the project completed in 8 months, while our initial estimate was 11 months. Based on a detailed analysis of the scope, I identified potential areas for acceleration. As a result of preparing a comprehensive report and meeting with the client, we agreed on a 10-month completion date with some scope modifications.

7. If a project team member consistently missed deadlines or did not complete their work to the required standard, how would you address the issue?

How to Answer: Emphasize direct and professional communication. Describe your approach to first understanding the root causes of the issue and then working with the team member to create an improvement plan, possibly involving additional resources or training.

Example: On a school construction project, a subcontractor was consistently delivering work late. I arranged a meeting with the subcontractor to understand the root causes of the delays. We discovered that his son's soccer practice was on Wednesday evening and it was nearly impossible to get a schedule update out by Thursday. We worked together to shift the process so updates would come out Friday morning. This approach was a win-win for us both and strengthened the relationship.

8. How would you develop the scheduling program for this company starting from scratch?

How to Answer: Developing a scheduling program needs to take into consideration the industry and the company (hopefully you've researched both). This is where you demonstrate your complete understanding of all project scheduling from preconstruction all the way through to delivery.

Example: In developing a construction scheduling program from scratch, I'd first collaborate closely with project managers and other key stakeholders to gain insights into the specific scheduling challenges posed by construction projects. Understanding construction phases, resource requirements, and critical paths would guide the development process. Gaining insights into what the program's goals are.

Using what I learned from those discussions, I would create a proposal that proposed a path forward for the company. The plan would include a set of goals, strategies, and tactics to achieve them, as well as an organizational strategy for achieving those goals. One key slide would be the timeline and set of deliverables.

After that, I'd focus on delivering the plan and communicating the status of establishing the program to project managers and key stakeholders.

9. If a project's scope changed mid-way through the schedule, how would you adapt the schedule to account for these changes?

How to Answer: Discuss your process of thoroughly reviewing the scope changes and analyzing their impact on the schedule. Emphasize your approach to updating the schedule, obtaining necessary approvals, and communicating the changes to all stakeholders.

Example: On a mixed-use development, the client decided to add a new floor. I revised the work in the schedule, re-evaluated the critical path, and forecasted the new completion date. I created a comprehensive analysis that summarized the changes and provided additional backup. This was to the stakeholders and I ensured we obtained their buy-in on the revised date and budget.

10. If a contractor informed you that they would be unable to complete their work on time, how would you adjust the schedule to minimize the impact on the project timeline?

How to Answer: Explain that you would assess the delay's impact on the overall project timeline, identify potential areas where time could be recovered, and consider alternative solutions. Those could include overtime, swing shifts, expediting material, eliminating scope, etc.

Example: When a key contractor was delayed due to an unforeseen labor strike, I immediately conducted an impact analysis and identified tasks that could be parallelized to recover some of the time. I also vetted alternative lead times for equipment and negotiated a new timeline, keeping the overall project only one week behind schedule instead of 3 months.

11. If a project experienced unexpected delays due to weather or other external factors, how would you manage the schedule to keep the project on track?

How to Answer: Emphasize your proactive approach to risk management, adaptive scheduling, and effective communication with stakeholders. Explain how you would have built in a process for handling weather delay in the contractual process.

Example: After a severe storm delayed a data center project, I promptly organized a risk assessment meeting with the team. I ensured the process for weather days was extremely clear when establishing the project. We identified the delayed tasks and determined that a contingency day was justified. Having reported our findings to stakeholders, I explained that we were taking all possible measures to minimize the delay's impact, but that for now we needed to use the contingency day. We were able to approve it without spending too much time or causing lots of churn.

12. If you discovered an error in the project schedule after it had been approved and distributed, how would you correct the error and communicate the changes to the project team?

How to Answer: Highlight your commitment to integrity and transparency, and your process for quickly updating the schedule and communicating the correction to all stakeholders. Provide a process to prevent how an error like this could happen in the future.

Example: I discovered a critical path error in a base schedule the day after it was submitted. I immediately called a meeting with the project team to explain the error. As soon as we gained alignment, we informed stakeholders of the error, explained the corrections, and distributed the updated schedule. In order to prevent future errors like this, I needed to learn how to prevent them. We had compartmentalized offline reviews within project groups, but we needed one final deep dive review. A standard process was created and added to our standard checklist.

13. If a project was running behind schedule and needed to be expedited, what steps would you take to speed up the schedule while still ensuring quality work?

How to Answer: Describe your ability to perform schedule compression techniques. Explore alternatives like fast tracking, crashing, overtime, expediting, etc. Ensure you weigh these decisions against potential risks and costs.

Example: For a hotel project that fell behind due to supplier issues, I implemented a crashing strategy by bringing in additional skilled labor and adjusting work sequences. While this increased costs slightly, we met the critical deadline for the grand opening. The strategy was so effective that I added to the standard delivery strategy so it could be used on future projects.

14. Tell me about a time when you had to negotiate with stakeholders to reach a mutually beneficial outcome.

How to Answer: Illustrate your negotiation skills and your ability to find compromises that satisfy conflicting interests while maintaining the project's objectives.

Example: The client for a residential complex was pushing for higher-end finishes that would have significantly increased costs and extended the timeline. I arranged a meeting with the client and our team to explore various options, and we negotiated a mix of high-end finishes in key areas and more budget-friendly options elsewhere. This met the client's quality expectations while keeping the project within budget and on schedule.

15. Describe a time when you had to manage conflicting priorities and how you handled the situation.

How to Answer: Share an example where you had to balance competing demands and how you prioritize work based on critical factors like deadlines, risk, or strategic importance.

Example: During a large hospital project, we were simultaneously in the final phase of one building and the initial phase of another. Both were claiming priority for resources. I led a planning session with project managers from both buildings and we developed a resource allocation plan that prioritized the final phase of the first building, while efficiently starting work on the second. This ensured the first building could be delivered and occupied while keeping the second on track for its milestones.

Technical Questions

16. How do you create a project schedule, and what factors do you consider when developing one?

How to Answer: The person wants to know how you build a construction schedule. Since this is very open ended, start by asking questions. Describe the key factors you consider first. Finally, a high level overview of how to schedule is created. Be sure not to get lost in details and ramble for 20 minutes about lags.

Example: Building a project scale is no easy task. The most important factors to consider when building are the scope, the contract, the location of the project and an understanding why the project is being built. By deeply understanding these factors, it will increase the likelihood of building a successful schedule.

Would you mind if I asked what's the project I'm building a schedule for? What kind of contract does it support? Where is it located in the world? Why are we building it?

Now that I have a better understanding of the project. My first step would be to create a high level milestone schedule. We will expand on this, but at the current point of the project, there isn't enough detail to be useful. To create a first draft, I would gather historical data, industry standards, and consult with the project management team. I would then hold a workshop to develop a Level 2 schedule based on this first draft. The number of activities would range from 20 to 50. As a result, the team will be able to plan their design, purchase early long lead equipment, and demonstrate the initial flow of construction. The schedule will be shared with the team after the workshop for comment. As more design was completed, we'd update the schedule with regular progress updates.

Do you want me to elaborate more on any of the process or the schedule?

17. What is critical path analysis, and how do you use it to optimize project timelines?

How to Answer: Explain that critical path analysis is a technique used to identify the longest path through the project with the least amount of float. Describe how it helps determine the minimum duration for the entire project and how you use it to identify critical activities. Point out potential pitfalls.

Example: The critical path is the fastest point from the start to the finish of the project. First, it's important to verify whether the critical paths are accurate using P6. You can achieve this by looking at the scope and design. The project team members would also be reviewed by me. As soon as trust is built into the critical path, it's important to track and actively work to derisk items. I found commissioning the electrical equipment to be the most critical part of my latest data center project. Since permanent power wasn't available, I recommended adding temporary power to remove it from the critical path. This added 3 weeks of float to that path. After that, we followed the next path and the next one.

18. How do you track project progress and identify potential delays or issues?

How to Answer: Stress your active tracking of project advancement compared to the initial schedule. Specify the techniques and tools you employ, including software and communication methods.

Example: Maintaining project progress and promptly identifying any issues or delays is pivotal to on time delivery. To accomplish this, I adopt a proactive approach by employing the following methods:

I ensure there is a standard well understood progressing method. Hopefully we can deploy a standard rules credit to reduce physical % ambiguity. The next important component are effective progress meetings. This direct interaction aids in identifying emerging issues and solutions collaboratively.

After progress is captured I'm looking to provide insights into task completion rates, enabling a comprehensive view of progress. Additionally, I conduct frequent progress meetings to discuss updates and address potential roadblocks.

I'll additionally try to walk the job site at least once a month to compare the progress in the schedule to what I can physically see. If there's a disconnect there, we have a problem.

Any issue is flagged and handled with the correct project team member. If big enough, I'll escalate to the project director.

19. Can you define free float and total float?

How to Answer: Free float is the amount of time an activity can be delayed without delaying the early start of its successor. Total float is the amount of time an activity can be delayed without delaying the project completion date.

Example: In a project I managed, Activity A had a free float of 5 days, meaning we could delay it by up to 5 days without affecting the subsequent activities. The total float was 7 days, indicating the flexibility we had before the project completion date was impacted.

20. What are some of the key performance indicators (KPIs) that you use to measure project schedule performance?

How to Answer: Mention common KPIs like Schedule Variance (SV), Schedule Performance Index (SPI), Critical Path Length Index (CPLI), and Baseline Execution Index (BEI).

Example: I regularly track SPI to assess how efficiently the project team is using time, and CPLI to understand the efficiency of the project's critical path. While no metric is perfect these have been helpful in the past. For example, on a school library project the SPI for the foundation started to dip below 1. I deep dived into the quantity tracking and realized that the subcontractor was even more behind than the schedule had indicated. I flagged this with the project management and noted that a double shift could make up the delay. We were able to bring in those additional resources and get the project back on track.

21. What are the constraints in Primavera P6?

How to Answer: Discuss the different types of constraints in Primavera P6, such as Start No Earlier Than, Finish No Later Than, Mandatory Start, and Mandatory Finish.

22. What is a WBS?

How to Answer: Explain that a Work Breakdown Structure (WBS) is a hierarchical decomposition of the total scope of work to be carried out by the project team. Mention there is a structure built into P6 however there can also be other project WBS to align a variety of systems. These can be accommodated with activity codes.

23. What is an open-ended activity in Primavera?

How to Answer: An open-ended activity in Primavera is an activity that does not have a successor (no 'Finish to Start' relationship with another activity).

Example: In a recent project, an open-ended activity was the client's final inspection – it had no successor since it was the final step before project closeout.

24. What is an S curve?

How to Answer: Describe an S curve as a visual tool displaying cumulative project data plotted against time. Emphasize its role in providing insights into project progress and performance.

Example: An S curve is a graphical depiction that presents cumulative project data, such as costs or work hours, plotted against the project's timeline. This curve resembles the shape of the letter 'S' and is a valuable instrument for visually representing project progress and performance trends.

For instance, during a highway construction project, I effectively utilized an S curve to compare the planned progress with the actual progress achieved over time. By doing so, stakeholders gained a clear visual understanding of whether the project was on track, ahead of schedule, or facing potential delays. The S curve's straightforward representation enabled quicker decision-making and adjustments when necessary, contributing to the project's overall success.

25. If given a project schedule, how would you go about reviewing it?

How to Answer: Describe a comprehensive approach to reviewing a project schedule. Detail specific aspects you would examine, such as logic, critical path, activity durations, resource allocations, constraints, and risk assessments.

Example: It is essential to review a project schedule to ensure a reliable forecast. To conduct a thorough review, I follow a comprehensive process that encompasses the following key aspects:

In the first place, I check that the basic contract requirements have been met. Things like contractual dates and coding.

Next, I carefully examine the schedule's logic. The sequence of activities must make sense and follow a logical progression. Identifying activities that are out of sequence or may lead to conflicts is crucial.

The next step is to identify the critical path accurately. The critical path determines the overall duration of a project based on the sequence of tasks. Understanding which tasks directly impact the project timeline depends on identifying the critical path correctly.

After the critical path I validate the estimate of the duration of activities. Based on historical data, industry benchmarks, and expert input, I verify these estimates. An accurate schedule can be achieved by making sure that activity durations are reasonable and well-founded.

Verify that the design, procurement, and equipment sub schedules are aligned with the current plan. There can be major problems if others are marching to a different drum.

Lastly, I pay close attention to risk assessments incorporated into the schedule. This involves identifying potential risks that could impact the project and assessing how these risks are accounted for in the schedule. To mitigate potential delays and disruptions, effective risk management strategies are essential.

As an example of my expertise, I reviewed the schedule of a recent hospital construction project. Obtaining regulatory approvals was identified as a critical activity that was not initially on the critical path. I realized its impact on the project's overall timeline and resource allocation during my review. Recalibrating the schedule to reflect this resulted in a more accurate representation of the project's timeline and better preparation for potential delays.

26. What is SV, CV, SPI, and CPI?

How to Answer: SV (Schedule Variance) indicates how much the schedule is ahead or behind the planned schedule. CV (Cost Variance) is a measure of cost performance in a project. SPI (Schedule Performance Index) is a measure of schedule efficiency. CPI (Cost Performance Index) is a measure of cost efficiency.

Example: In a project, I calculated the SPI as 1.05, indicating we were progressing at 105% of the rate originally planned, thus we were ahead of schedule. The CPI was 0.98, indicating that we were slightly over budget.

IMPACT IDEAS

The following ideas can help you generate impact on your project or program. If you are looking for a raise or promotion, or if you are looking to add work experience to your resume, these are great ideas.

Improve the schedule submission process.

Establish what a standard submission contains. Create examples of each document, report and data included. Build a calendar to document critical dates in the process (Progress updated, Date Submitted, Comments Returned, Accepted, etc.) Develop quality checks to ensure files meet the standards. Set up a scoreboard that ranks each submission. Track submission performance.

Create a standard process for reviewing schedule submissions.

Create a list of specific criteria. Define each criteria and create a score. Create a "How To" document that demonstrates how to review the schedule and score the criteria. Create tools to help with the review like developing, specific Primavera P6 layouts, export spreadsheets, reports etc. Measure the time it takes to review and work to improve that time.

Implement KPIs (key performance indicators) for project scheduling.

Determine which metrics are applicable. Consider KPIs like schedule variance, critical path changes, activity starts and finishes, float, etc. Work with the project team to determine what is most applicable. Build the first draft of KPI's in excel. Get alignment on the calculations, the definitions and acceptable scoring ranges. Work to create an automated dashboard to track these KPIs in real-time. Build easily understood visuals. Train team members on how to interpret and act on KPI data. Regularly review and adjust KPIs to align with project and company goals.

Master Primavera P6 and Scheduling Tools.

Create a standard process for learning Primavera P6. Start by creating a list of key functionalities to master, including critical features such as scheduling techniques, resource leveling, and cost management. Define each functionality and create a learning scorecard to break down each feature into sub-skills, rating your proficiency (e.g., beginner, intermediate, advanced). Develop a "How To" document with detailed learning paths and resources, compiling tutorials, videos, and guides that cover each functionality in depth. Create customized layouts and reports in P6, such as templates that streamline common tasks like baseline comparisons and variance reports. Measure your proficiency regularly and set improvement goals by tracking your progress with periodic self-assessments and adjusting your learning plan accordingly.

Setup a Lunch and Learn Series.

Setup a once a month meeting that dives into a specific topic. Determine the first 3 or 4 topics. The topics could be technology, a process review, a book club, a speaker, etc. Invite people who you think would be interested. Ask management to cover food. Take pictures of the event. Send out a quick email after each session.

Create a career progression plan.

Outline a 1-year, 3-year, and 5-year plan with specific milestones and goals. Define the skills and experiences needed for each step, identifying necessary skills, certifications, and job experiences for advancement. Share with your manager and mentor for feedback. Create a tracking tool for career progress using a spreadsheet to monitor your achievements and goals. Measure your progress regularly by reviewing and updating your career plan quarterly to ensure you stay on track. Share your progress with your manager regularly.

Build a planning and scheduling tool roadmap.

Develop a comprehensive planning and scheduling tool roadmap. Start by conducting a thorough assessment of your current scheduling tools and processes. Identify gaps and areas for improvement by gathering feedback from team members and stakeholders. Research different tools and potential creation opportunities. Use this information to create a detailed roadmap that outlines the steps for implementing new tools or upgrading existing ones. The roadmap could include timelines, resource allocation, training plans, and success metrics. After gaining team alignment, present this roadmap to senior management.

Establish a focus group or team on improving productivity predictability.

Determine the areas on the project or program that suffer the most from lack of predictability. Implement systems to monitor, track root causes of miss and enhance the predictability of task completion.. Use this data to target specific areas for improvement, such as different sequencing, providing additional planning training, or resources to underperforming teams.

Take initiative in managing without formal authority.

Identify opportunities within your current role where you can lead small teams or projects. For example, volunteer to spearhead a task force aimed at improving existing scheduling processes. Clearly define goals, delegate tasks, and regularly review progress with the team. By demonstrating your leadership skills and ability to manage without formal authority, you'll build a strong case for your capability to handle more significant responsibilities.

Engage stakeholders to build a scheduling culture.

Conduct an assessment to evaluate the current scheduling culture across all stakeholders, including owners, general contractors, and subcontractors. Use both quantitative metrics (such as schedule submission timeliness and adherence to standards) and qualitative metrics (like team perceptions and usefulness of scheduling tools) to gain a comprehensive understanding. Share your findings and create actionable plans to address any issues, fostering a collaborative environment that values scheduling as a critical component of project success.

Create a recognition program.

Regularly acknowledge the achievements of team members who embrace and contribute positively to scheduling practices. This could involve sending appreciation emails to their managers, organizing small celebrations like team lunches, or implementing recognition programs such as "Scheduler of the Month." Regularly highlight and celebrate the achievements of high performers to motivate the entire team and foster a culture of excellence.

Integrate risk management into the scheduling process.

Create a presentation explaining the benefits of performing risk management and a high level overview of the process. Run a pilot and conduct a quantitative risk analysis (QSRA) to evaluate the impact of potential delays and cost overruns. Develop risk mitigation strategies to address key risk drivers, such as late design package releases or external factors like weather events and inflation. Train your team and project managers on risk management best practices, emphasizing the importance of proactive risk identification and mitigation. Embedding risk management into your scheduling process, you will enhance project predictability and reliability.

Develop a team definition and dictionary.

Begin by identifying key terms, phrases, and concepts that are critical to your team's success. Create a document that defines each term and provides context for its use. Share the document and encourage others to contribute. Consider creating prizes for people who contribute the most. Have a ranking system to determine which terms are the most helpful and used.

Establish a mentoring program for new schedulers.

Pair new hires with experienced team members who can provide guidance and support. Develop a structured mentoring plan that includes regular check-ins, goal setting, and progress reviews. Provide mentors with training on how to effectively coach and support their mentees. This program will help new team members acclimate quickly, build their skills, and feel supported, ultimately improving retention and performance.

Set up a continuous improvement team.

Form a dedicated team responsible for identifying and implementing improvements to scheduling and planning processes. Encourage team members to submit ideas for improvements and provide a structured process for evaluating and implementing these ideas. Regularly review the impact of implemented changes and adjust as needed. Build a roadmap that highlights current improvements being worked on and what improvements are next. This continuous improvement approach will help keep your processes efficient and effective, driving ongoing success.

Build a cross-functional collaboration framework.

Develop a strategy for improving collaboration between different departments and teams within your organization. Schedule regular cross-functional meetings to discuss ongoing projects, share updates, and address any challenges. Create communication channels that facilitate easy sharing of information and resources. By fostering strong collaboration, you can ensure that all teams are aligned and working towards common goals, improving overall project outcomes.

Implement Earned Value Management (EVM) effectively.

Begin by clearly defining the purpose and benefits of EVM for your organization. Conduct in-person presentations and roadshows to explain the implementation process, ensuring engagement and understanding. Highlight how EVM will help track planned versus actual progress, identify potential cost overruns early, and ultimately prevent delays and budget issues. Standardize EVM processes across projects. Develop a template schedule with standardized codes and structures that can be used across all projects. This ensures consistency and ease of understanding as team members move between projects. Incorporate both high-level packages and detailed activities, making sure the schedule aligns with estimating data for accurate tracking of labor and costs.

Implement a systematic benchmarking process across projects.

Begin by gathering comprehensive data from previous projects, focusing on the key elements such as scope, duration, and cost. Analyze this data to identify patterns and variances in performance. Focus on items that performed well and items that performed poorly. Use this benchmarking data to establish baseline metrics and identify systematic issues that can be addressed to improve overall project predictability and performance. Develop a process to refresh the benchmarking data with each new project and set of data.

Establish a production planning or pull planning system for near-term planning.

Create a collaborative environment where tasks are planned and executed efficiently. Develop a visual timeline with milestones, task dependencies, and resource allocations. Conduct regular planning meetings to review progress and make adjustments. Establish standard operating procedures (SOPs) for the planning process, including guidelines on task sequencing, resource management, and risk mitigation. Create a 'How To' manual with examples and best practices. Measure the effectiveness of your planning system with metrics like schedule adherence and productivity rates. Identify and address inefficiencies in the current process, proposing and implementing solutions that save time and resources.

Establish real-time progress tracking and monitoring.

Utilize advanced technologies and tools, such as augmented reality platforms, to enable live progress tracking. This allows for accurate, real-time data collection and helps identify issues as they arise. Integrate these tools with existing scheduling software to streamline progress updates and reporting, ensuring that all stakeholders have access to up-to-date information.

Create a focus on early detection and intervention of problems.

These can be from the initial planning of the project, preconstruction, construction or commissioning. Implement processes that allow for early detection of issues and prompt intervention to address them. This includes regular progress reviews, variance analyses and escalation. Develop standard escalation paths for issues based on criticality, money and schedule. By identifying and addressing issues early, you can prevent them from causing significant delays or cost overruns.

Develop a dynamic knowledge management system that captures and utilizes construction project data efficiently.

Planners and schedulers should focus on establishing a system that aggregates all project-related data into a centralized, accessible knowledge graph. This system would include data from various sources like schedules, budgets, workforce details, and project outcomes, interlinked to provide comprehensive insights. By enabling better data connectivity and accessibility, the system would facilitate faster decision-making and more precise forecasting. Showcasing the ability to manage and leverage big data effectively can position planners and schedulers as vital assets to their organizations, making them prime candidates for advancement.

Initiate a proactive training program aimed at equipping team members with skills in emerging technologies and methodologies in construction planning.

Lead the creation and implementation of workshops or online courses focusing on digital tools, data analytics, and machine learning applications in construction. This initiative not only increases the overall competency of the team but also highlights leadership and commitment to organizational growth. By fostering an environment of continuous learning and adaptation, planners and schedulers can enhance their visibility and influence within the company, improving their prospects for raises and promotions.

Develop concise and impactful project updates.

Start by summarizing the key points and decisions needed from the executive team. Create clear, visually appealing charts that differentiate between actuals, forecasts, and baselines. Build a template that is easy for everyone on the team to fill out and present. Ensure your updates focus on actionable insights rather than overwhelming details. By presenting clear, concise, and relevant information, you demonstrate your ability to manage and communicate project statuses effectively, increasing your visibility and credibility within the organization.

Establish a production planning or pull planning system for near-term planning.

Learn the principles and methodology of the Last Planner System (LPS). Start with a pilot and implement a collaborative planning system using LPS to ensure reliable project execution. Begin by creating a master schedule with clear milestones with all stakeholders, then work backward from deadlines to ensure task readiness. Make-ready planning meetings use a look-ahead plan for upcoming tasks to identify and remove constraints. Measure performance using the Percent Plan Complete (PPC) metric and hold weekly planning meetings to track promises. Utilize daily huddles for immediate task reviews and learning sessions to reflect on performance and improve continuously. Using these steps enhances collaboration and accountability, demonstrating leadership and commitment, thereby increasing your chances of a raise or promotion.

Establish a standard time impact analysis process.

First, identify all the steps necessary to conduct a thorough time impact analysis (TIA). Document each step in a detailed procedure manual to ensure clarity and comprehensiveness. Ensure consistency in methodology by developing specific templates and checklists for collecting and analyzing data, such as impact event logs, time impact schedules, and narrative reports. Utilize software such as Primavera P6 to create consistent TIAs. Use real project examples to illustrate best practices and common pitfalls. Train your team on the standardized process. Based on feedback and lessons learned from completed analyses, regularly review and refine your TIA process. Establishing and continuously improving this process will help you demonstrate your expertise and reliability, enabling you to be a valuable asset to your organization.

Enhance your presentation skills.

Practice your project update presentations to ensure clarity, confidence, and professionalism. Focus on delivering your message with precision and brevity, and be prepared to answer detailed questions from executives. Consider taking courses or workshops on public speaking and presentation skills to further refine your abilities. By consistently delivering polished and impactful presentations, you build trust with stakeholders and position yourself as a capable leader, paving the way for potential raises and promotions.

Perform a comprehensive risk assessment.

Conduct a thorough risk analysis covering schedule, cost, health and safety, and commercial risks. For each risk, determine the potential impact and likelihood, then model different scenarios using tools like Monte Carlo simulations. Present this data clearly, showing both the best and worst-case outcomes, and propose mitigation strategies. Ensure your presentation includes detailed visuals that are easy to understand, like clear charts and graphs. By providing a complete picture of the risks and your plan to manage them, you will demonstrate your strategic thinking and ability to safeguard project success.

Introduce performance-based incentives that reward predictability and quality in project delivery.

For example, tie contractor and subcontractor bonuses to their ability to meet deadlines, maintain safety standards, and identify innovative ways to improve processes. This could involve providing a portion of their compensation based on project milestones or specific performance metrics, such as on-time delivery and safety compliance. By aligning incentives with project goals, you encourage behaviors that drive better outcomes, enhancing your reputation and increasing the likelihood of repeat business from satisfied clients.

Develop an equipment purchasing tracking system to streamline procurement and ensure timely project execution.

Establish a centralized database to log all equipment purchase orders, including supplier details, lead times, and expected delivery dates. Create a standardized procedure for entering and updating purchase information to maintain data accuracy. Implement a system to track and compare lead times from different suppliers, identifying the most reliable options.

Adopt Critical Chain Method.

Explore and implement advanced scheduling and execution methods, such as Critical Chain Project Management (CCPM), to improve project reliability and reduce overall duration and costs. CCPM focuses on managing project uncertainties by prioritizing the critical path and actively managing buffers. Train your project teams on these methods and integrate them into your project management practices. By using these advanced techniques, you can achieve more predictable and efficient project outcomes, setting your organization apart as a forward-thinking and capable contractor.

Develop comprehensive schedule templates in Primavera P6.

Start by identifying the common project types your team handles and create a Work Breakdown Structure (WBS) for each type. Define and include all necessary activity codes to categorize and filter activities effectively. Assign typical resources required for each activity, ensuring that labor, equipment, and materials are considered. Establish standard sequences and durations based on historical data and industry best practices, creating logical relationships between activities. Document this template creation process thoroughly, including a step-by-step guide on how to utilize the templates in future projects. Regularly review and update these templates to reflect any changes in processes, resources, or project requirements. By doing so, you will streamline project planning, enhance consistency, and demonstrate your value in optimizing project scheduling.

Establish and share a comprehensive calendar of key events.

Identify all crucial milestones and deadlines, including schedule submissions, pay application deadlines, report due dates, and meetings. Use project management or calendar software to input these dates, ensuring accessibility and regular updates. Set reminders for upcoming events to avoid missed deadlines. Communicate the calendar clearly to all team members and stakeholders, ensuring awareness of responsibilities and timelines. Regularly review and adjust the calendar as project dynamics change, maintaining accuracy. This proactive approach enhances coordination, accountability, and overall project success.

Develop a database to track changes to major milestones.

Keep track of the original dates, the changes, and the rationale behind those changes. Maintain a detailed log within the database for each milestone, its original date, and any changes. Update the database regularly with new information and review it to identify patterns or recurring issues. Make sure it is easy to enter and retrieve data. Build a chart to visually highly change over time. Ensure it is accessible to all relevant team members.

How to Become a Unicorn

In the world of planning and scheduling, a unicorn is someone with unparalleled expertise, commanding top-tier compensation, and is highly sought after. So, how do you become a unicorn planner There isn't a one-size-fits-all approach. To help you grow your horn, here are 6 strategies:

1. Deep Knowledge of the Foundations and Understanding of Adjacent Areas

The list is extensive: planning, scheduling, project controls, estimating, contracting, permitting, engineering and design, procurement, construction methodologies, commissioning, prefabrication, system integrations, various software, tools, etc. What separates unicorns? Because of their love of learning, they connect the dots holistically.

2. Skill Specialization: Collect Niches to Become World Class

Unicorns are unique. You can't become one by having the same skill set and experience as everyone else. Once you've gained a deep knowledge of the foundations, you'll have to find what can set you apart. Maybe you picked up programming, prompting, or learned to speak Mandarin. Follow your passions and add another skill. These skills make you one of a kind but also have a tremendous impact on projects.

3. Eagerly Take on Responsibilities to Create Impact

For their next step, unicorns always gather the right experiences. They're efficient dynamos, taking tasks that took others days and accomplishing them in hours. This efficiency lets them shoulder more responsibility because they create time. In their work, they combine surefire solutions with moonshots.

4. Possess a Storytelling Knack

You'd better be good at explaining your existence if you were a mythical creature! It is rare for executives to want to see a detailed Gantt chart. At most, you might present 4 to 5 bars. Unicorns convey messages like captivating short stories. They're the first to be called for major meetings when plans need explaining. Not just with executives—unicorns thrive in boots-on-the-ground discussions, pinpointing and solving core issues that delay projects.

5. Establish Strong Networking Circles and Pursue Mentorship

Guidance, shared experiences, and navigating industry challenges are invaluable. Unicorns recognize the power of a robust network and mentorship in speeding growth. What's a great way to get started? Give back to the communities that supported their journey. Help a junior unicorn on the way.

6. Recognize Your Worth

The unicorns recognize their worth as their credentials grow and their expertise shines. They're bold and ready to take advantage of incredible opportunities others might think are beyond their reach. They aren't afraid to move on when they've learned all they can from a role.

Remember, as you close this book, that success, happiness, and a successful career aren't just dreams but deliberate choices and actions. Keep refining your skills and pushing beyond conventional boundaries to grow your earnings.

Ensure your work brings joy and rewards by aligning it with your values and passions. Embrace the confidence that each step you take leads to a fulfilling career. You'll learn how to survive and thrive in the competitive world of construction scheduling and planning.

Using the knowledge and strategies in this book, you will be among the top 1%, making more money, living a fulfilling life, and reaching career success.

See you at the top.

9 7 9 8 3 3 0 4 6 4 5 6 2